The High Road
A Kid's Guide To Edinburgh In Scotland

Photography By John D. Weigand
Poetry By Penelope Dyan

Bellissima Publishing, LLC
Jamul, California
www.bellissimapublishing.com

copyright © 2011 by Penny D. Weigand and John D. Weigand

All rights reserved. No part of this book may be reproduced or transmitted in any form or by any means, electronic or mechanical, including photocopying, recording, or by any other means, or by any information or storage retrieval system, without permission from the publisher.

ISBN 978-1-61477-013-8
First Edition

To bagpipes and drums, and a life not ho-hum!

The High Road

Bellissima Publishing, LLC

Introduction

Edinburgh in Scotland is a delightful place where lightness and darkness combine and fuel the imagination. There is a castle standing on an ominous hill and a spire that reminds us of wizards and all sorts of possibly scary things. This is where Photographer John D. Weigand and attorney, award winning author, and former educator, Penelope Dyan, whisk you away with thoughts of time past. As usual, Weigand and Dyan are not about a bunch of facts, but rather they are about exploring thoughts, and growing through discovery. They capture what a child will see, and encourage children to add to these travel books with their own thoughts and writings, and photographs, tickets and things; because this is how children learn, and this is how they can make both the book and the learning experience and process their very own!

Penelope Dyan (as a former teacher) knows just how to do this. Whether you travel vicariously with Weigand and Dyan, through the pages of this book, or you take an actual trip, the process is the same. Add to the book and makes some discoveries of your own! Enjoy the photographs and the poetry in this made for kids book! Take the High Road!

The High Road
A Kid's Guide To Edinburgh In Scotland

Photography By John D. Weigand
Poetry By Penelope Dyan

Antenna and chimneys
from shingled rooftops sprout,
when you are in Edinburgh in
Scotland, and you drive
all about!

You see the Edinburgh Castle high on a hill.
You watch the British flag in the sky as you stand oh so still.
The flag flutters above you in the clouds and in the wind.
It's where you want to go!
So your journey begins!

There are bagpipes and kilts!

There is a bus you can take!

There are flags!
There's a clock tower!

There is a blue dome,
for goodness sake!

There are windowsill flowers.

And stairs go up, up, to the hill.
Where you first saw that castle
as you stood oh so still!

You notice people resting.
Some have picnics on the grass.
Your tummy grumbles,
and so you walk VERY fast.

You pass the National Gallery
of Scotland,
and as you proceed on your way,
Your mother exclaims
breathlessly,
"What a tiring, tiring day!"
You continue to climb to the
stairs' top,
but your mother wants to rest,
and so for a moment you stop.

When you arrive at the top
there's lots to see!
And things are much the same
as they ALWAYS used to be.
You see a church.
You order sandwiches to eat.
Desert is a cake, lemony sweet.

Tourists shop for shirts,
scarves, candy, maybe a kilt.
(Never flowers--they will wilt.)
The castle is a lot of fun!
And ahead of Mom and Dad
you and Sis' start to run.
Mom yells, "Don't run so fast!"
You say to your sis',
"Fun just does NOT last!"
Then you BOTH giggle. . .
and YOU buy a NEW toy,
that's perfect for a girl or boy!

O ye'll tak' the high road,
and I'll tak' the low road,
And I'll be in Scotland afore ye,
But me and my true love will never meet again,
On the bonnie, bonnie banks o' Loch Lomond.

Anonymous

www.ingramcontent.com/pod-product-compliance
Ingram Content Group UK Ltd.
Pitfield, Milton Keynes, MK11 3LW, UK
UKHW060135240426
12048UKWH00002B/42